Small Groups That Work

TEN SECRETS
TO LIFE-CHANGING
RELATIONSHIPS

MARK INGMIRE

Small Groups That Work: Ten Secrets To Life-Changing Relationships

This book is a work of love. The stories and secrets are based on the author's life experiences. All personal experiences mentioned are based on true stories and used for educational content and impact. I hope it not only helps with the quality of small group life, but in all relationships as well.

For more information, contact the author at mwingmire@gmail.com.

Book and Cover design by Ashley Gilbert

ISBN: 978-1-62888-530-9

Second Edition: June 2016

10 9 8 7 6 5 4 3 2

DEDICATION

To my wife, Margaret, who continually makes me better.

ACKNOWLEDGEMENTS

Thank you to Gina Tomlin, who was indispensable as my editor, and to Franz and Ashley Gilbert, who have opened new doors that I never knew existed.

CONTENTS

APPENDICES

Preface

There isn't a shortage of books and articles written about small groups, so, is there really a need for one more? Maybe not; however, the number of books written by someone who has years of experience successfully leading small groups and small groups ministry in the church are fewer. To give full disclosure, I need to mention that there was more than one failure among those years of success.

The purpose of this book is not to champion a certain small group model or discuss theory that has never been tried or tested for the long-haul. Instead, everything in this book is based on those years of experience that has been met with success. Even the stories used to illustrate every point in each chapter are true. Only the names have been changed to protect the innocent . . . and the guilty.

This book is also not about various spiritual disciplines every leader and every follower of Christ should embody. While those disciplines, such as prayer and daily devotional time, are critical to the health of the leader, this book's focus is on understanding in practical ways how God made you and me to relate with one another.

Understanding how God created us to function best in God-given community is just as important as the spiritual disciplines for which we strive. In fact, I would argue that how God created us to relate to each other in community is very much part of our spiritual formation.

Therefore, the purpose of this book is to take those years of experience to communicate the core skills of leading a life-changing small group. This book won't answer every question about small groups, but it will give you the foundation to lead a small group that has every chance of working. . . guaranteed!

Before we dive into the book's content, let me suggest a few ways this book can be used:

1. Read it from the beginning to the end to hone your own small group leading skills, even if you disagree with what's written. Sometimes it's the things we disagree with that help us learn the most.
2. Keep it close at hand as a resource to trouble-shoot when something in your group isn't working right.
3. Utilize this book for training small group leaders or small group coaches. Each chapter is short, so they could be read together in a training group setting. Then use the questions at the end of each chapter to process its application.
4. Memorize the 10 Secrets of Small Groups That Work. They are listed at the end of each chapter after the title, Key Phrase to Remember, and as a list in the appendix. Have your training group come to the first

class with the 10 Secrets already memorized and quiz them each time you meet. The quiz could be as simple as writing down each point word for word.

Maybe this fourth suggestion sounds a little extreme. However, consider the United Parcel Service (UPS) which requires all of their drivers be able to pass a 10 Laws of the Road Quiz by writing down from memory every rule of the road. New drivers *must* pass this test before they are able to drive a package car. Do you think it's effective? Research shows that UPS has been the leading private industry in driver safety for almost one hundred years. Their first driver's safety handbook was issued in 1917. They have been updating and improving their driver's training ever since. Now, I ask from an eternal perspective, would you rather deliver packages the rest of your life, or would you rather invest your life by partnering with God in changing lives? If you choose to memorize these principles, there is a sample quiz following the 10 principles in the appendix.

Regardless of how you use this book, my last recommendation to you is to relax and have fun going through this book knowing that your salvation doesn't depend on how much of this book you read. However, you never know when you may be partnering with God to bring someone to a saving relationship with Him because of what you may learn from this book.

As you read it, thank God that He made you and me in a mysteriously wonderful way so that we live and grow best when we live in community!

Chapter 1

Small Groups That Work

"Small groups don't work." I remember the first time I heard the statement. The words came from a pastor whom I thought would have been an advocate of small groups. Since that first time, I have heard that phrase spoken again and have read it in ministry related articles. I have to admit that when I first heard the statement, "Small groups don't work," I was stopped in my tracks. I began to wonder if I had been wrong about my belief in small groups being able to change lives. In fact, I felt compelled to spend time self-evaluating my past experiences with the groups I have led or of which I had been a part. I even spent time evaluating my own small groups ministries in an attempt to discern if small groups really do work. By working, I mean that one would expect to see spiritual and personal growth occur, knowledge of scripture increase, and Biblical community experienced. Since the title of this book is "Small Groups That Work," you can probably guess where I landed. After processing what I considered to be a disturbing statement, I concluded that small groups do work.

I have since learned when I hear "Small groups don't work" spoken, I have to ask some follow-up questions to understand why the statement was made. The answer is usually related to some basic dysfunction of small group life from that person's own small group experience. Sometimes the person had different expectations of and for the group, or someone promised more than what small groups were able to provide. Regardless of the reason for the group's apparent failure, the truth is that just because you form a small group doesn't mean it will work.

In the following pages I want to share with you some of the very basic, yet essential, practices of small groups that give them the ingredients to work! Leading a small group isn't rocket science. You don't have to be the brightest crayon in the box to have a group that changes lives. Take my word for it; if I were a crayon, some think my color would be gray. Leading a small group effectively comes down to doing the basics. I can't emphasize enough the importance of focusing on the basics of leading a small group. If you like sports, there's a great story that illustrates the importance of the basics. It's the story told of legendary football coach, Vince Lombardi, pulling his players together for their first team meeting of each season. To start the meeting he would walk to the front of the room, stand in silence for a moment, then hold up a football before his team and say, "Gentlemen, this is a football." As the story goes, Lombardi proceeds to share with his team the basics of the game. He would talk about the importance of the football itself. Afterwards, he would lead the team out to the field and show them the boundaries and the end zone. This was not a pointless exercise even for those who were seasoned veterans of the game. Every time he gave his speech, his players reported that they would learn something new as well as be reminded of what makes a football team successful. He saw that a lack of focusing on the basics kept his team from prevailing. Similarly, those words about focusing on the basics ring true for those who lead a small group.

Leading a small group that changes lives requires the leader to focus on the fundamentals of an effective small group. It's not hard, but it does take time, planning, and execution. The basics usually don't involve little details such as the how clever the discussion questions were or how grammatically correct or lofty the group prayer was. The basics pay the big dividends to the life-change process we hope will come from a small group. The chapters that follow focus on those basics. Don't be overly concerned about drilling down into the details or being a perfectionist with each one; rather, just practice them. As you do, you will become proficient with each and see growth happen over short and long periods of time. As you practice the basics, remember to have fun! Every once in a while you may disappoint someone in your group. Don't let that stop you. Get back up and keep moving forward. Don't take the group or yourself so seriously that the group becomes a burden to carry. Enjoy the process that takes place as you experience Biblically grounded relationships and growth.

For Discussion

1. What are other words synonymous to the word "basic"? In your opinion, at what point do basic skills become advance skills and why is that important to distinguish between the two?

2. From your experiences, what do you consider to be some of the basics regarding relationships and growth?

3. What are some specific things you hope to gain or questions answered by reading this book?

Chapter 2

Is It Really Rocket Science?

"You Don't Have to Be a Rocket Scientist to Launch a Small Group."

Ken and Vickie have started a new small group and did everything they could to launch it well. They came up with a list of friends to invite, set the date of the first meeting, sent out invitations, made follow up phone calls, and prepared the agenda for their first meeting. They had six friends accept their invitation to their small group and all six came to the first two meetings. However, from that point forward they had trouble getting everyone there on the same night. On many nights, no one showed up. Ken and Vickie fixed a meal and prepared the lesson every week and quickly became frustrated when their group members failed to show up. Realizing they had a challenge, they quickly called their small group coach who came to the next group meeting. Upon that coach's arrival, he began to sum up the issue that was keeping Ken's and Vickie's group from having a successful launch. He discovered that not only was there a strong pungent odor noticeably at the front door, but the dogs charged the foyer to welcome their house guests. Through the evening, the dogs were a constant distraction not to mention the breaks that Vickie took to take care of their six-month-old baby. While Ken and Vickie were a nice couple, they weren't able to launch a group that would sustain itself. The coach gently and directly told them what he saw as the issues to correct, but little did anyone know then that the group had already ended.

Starting a small group from scratch can make a person anxious since the possibility of failing always exists. As with Ken and Vickie, they had not considered some important logistical issues nor evaluated the launch with their small group. Here are simple steps that take the guesswork out of launching a new small group.

Step One – Find at least one person or couple to join you.

Recruit one person or couple to agree to join your small group and help you launch it. Once you have that person or couple, you have a small group! I know that number is smaller than the group you are hoping for, but it's the perfect start. Be sure it's someone you like, because that person or couple will be your core group and be instrumental in helping you launch and sticking with you.

Here are some questions you will want to discuss with that committed person or couple. Most of the below questions will need to be answered for your Small Group Covenant of which we will talk about soon.

1. Where will our Small Group meet?
2. How often will we meet?
3. Will we provide childcare?
4. Will we organize dinner, snacks or nothing at all?
5. What topic or book of the Bible might we like to study?
6. Who do we want to invite?
7. When do we want to hold our first group meeting?

If you are not able to find someone to help you get started, not to worry. Move on to step two.

Our group will meet . . .
Where: _____
Day: _____   Time: _____
We'll handle food in the following way: _____
_____
Possible study: _____   ' _____
Date of first meeting: _____

Step Two – Make a list of people and invite them to join your small group.

With your core couple or individual, write down a list of people you want to invite. Plan to invite more than your home can hold since some will probably not be able to join your small group due to other commitments. Here's a simple way I learned from my friend, Kent Odor, to build your list. There are five circles of influence with whom you already have relationships. Consider each of the five areas as you put together your invitation list. The five areas of influence are: Friends, Family, Factory, Fun and Fellowship.

1. **Friends** are those you know in your neighborhood, at the local stores you do business with, those you went to school with, and the list could go on.

2. **Family** are the members of your family who live close enough to you that they could be an active part of your group.

3. **Factory** helps you to think of those you work with and would like for them to join your small group.

4. **Fun** are the people with whom you play sports, board games, biking, hiking or anything you do just for fun.

5. **Fellowship** includes the people with whom you go to the weekend worship services.

Now that you have your first meeting scheduled, work with your core group and the list you have created. Decide how you will invite those on your list to your first scheduled meeting. You can use most any method to invite these folks: email, mailed invitation, or phone call. If you invite by email, I would recommend putting everyone's email address in the "blind carbon copy" (bcc) address line since not everyone may want to share their email address with possible strangers. The same is true with texts. Not everyone wants to share their phone number with other people, so if you text the invitation, do each one individually. If you know what study or activities are being planned, include that information in the invitation. People are more likely to commit if they know to what they are committing themselves.

Also, be sure to set a deadline for their RSVP's, and if you don't hear from them, follow-up with a phone call.

With your core group and the date for your group's first actual meeting, plan that meeting's agenda. Plan to make this first meeting something relaxing and fun such as a cookout. This first meeting should give everyone who comes a chance to get to know each other and to talk about the plans for the small group. It's usually best to have the group's first study already determined so that you can talk about the group's plans. You can decide which study to do with the help of your core group.

Step Three – Determine if your small group will coordinate childcare during group meetings.

How you handle childcare can be one of the most important decisions as well as most difficult challenges your small group will face. While there are options on how to handle childcare, the list is not endless. Here are a few of the basic options that don't rely on the church to provide any support or compensation for childcare.

1. **The Sink or Swim Option.** Every parent in the group is responsible for getting their own childcare. The parents are responsible for providing a place where the baby-sitter would watch the children. The advantage to this approach is that the parents most likely have a trusted sitter. In addition, the sitter is also familiar with the children and their routine.

   The sitter could care for the children in either the parent's home or in the sitter's home. Regardless of where the children are cared for, the safety of the children come first. Not only is the safety of the children important, but making sure the sitter has a safe environment to serve as well.

2. **The Paid Childcare Option.** The small group could consider pooling resources to hire a sitter to watch the children. A suggestion would be to offer the sitter $2 or $3 dollar per child/family per group meeting. Some groups may offer more compensation, but it's important to not break the parent's bank. This option is usually cheaper than the "Sink or Swim" option.

   However, it is also comes with additional challenges. There are probably more children in the mix which give opportunities for conflict and increased disruptions with the group time. Therefore, it is important that the small group leader spends time with the group covering expectations for childcare and the sitter. The wise small group leader who chooses this option will spend the time for the first month after each group meeting to talk with the parents and how they felt childcare went the week before and that night. There is a childcare evaluation in the appendix as a tool to help you and your group move through the childcare challenge.

3. **The Group Members Rotate Option.** Every meeting someone from the group watches the other group members' children at the host home. This is the cheapest option for childcare of the first three options. It also has it's own challenges as well as it's own advantages. The larger the group the easier the rotation schedule can be on the small group. However, if the group is small, a group member may be out of the small group meeting two or more times in a month.

Another advantage of this approach is that the group member is able to speak into the life of children and build a relationship with the entire family and not just the parents.

4. **The Children are Group Members Option.** If the children are older, include them as group members. This option does away with the need for childcare. The small group can include the children in their Bible study time and even prayer time.

The advantage to this option is that the children are exposed to Bible teaching and the how to live life in community. After all, our faith in Christ is more caught than it is taught. I know my children loved the small group of which my wife and I were a part. To this day, as adults, they both attend their own small groups and even lead a small group for teenagers.

The optimum condition for childcare is that you do everything to keep the children and childcare workers safe. After the first two or three group meetings, gather the parents together for a brief meeting to ask how they thought childcare went and make any adjustments as necessary.

Step Four – Plan the agenda of your first meeting to include the following: ice breaker activity, Bible study, prayer and group business.

There are at least three things you will want to accomplish in your first meeting:

1. Emphasize relationship building by using fun or icebreaker activities. It's hard to have meaningful discussions with a stranger. Building relationships is a key building block for spiritual growth.

2. Plan a fellowship or social event. This could be held the same time your group normally would meet, or it could be another time and place altogether. Nothing accelerates relationship building quicker than to have a group outing or social. Again, this will help foster spiritual growth as you learn and serve one another.

3. Plan to introduce the small group covenant with the group. There is a covenant in the back of this book in the appendices. Every small group has a covenant. It's always better to have one that is understood clearly by everyone in the group. Use it, but don't become its slave. The covenant can be changed, but when everyone understands what the guidelines and values are, the group will be stronger.

Step Five – Prepare your home to host your small group.

Make sure you give as much attention to the host home as you have to the agenda. Set the room with chairs in a circle as much as possible and not in rows. A detail many group leaders may not consider is the height of the chairs. Ideally, it's best for group interaction to have the chairs as much as possible on the same height level. With people sitting on the floor and then on bar stools, conversation still happens, but it becomes more difficult to have good eye contact and the ability to observe subtle gestures that complete the process of conversing become more challenging.

Make sure there are plenty of supplies so that everyone can participate and be successful as they engage with the small group. These supplies include simple things like pens and pencils, nametags, Bibles and study guides. Group meetings go much better when these are already out and in place. Interrupting the meeting to go find these supplies when they are needed can be very disruptive, especially in serious and life-changing moments of group interaction.

Be sure any part of the home that could be used is cleaned and prepared. One of the biggest areas neglected by hosts is not to have more lights turned on. Turn on the porch light if it's dark outside; turn on the hall and bathroom lights so guests will know where the bathroom is. Also, make sure your bathroom is adequately prepared and equipped. More than one small group leader has shared with me stories of items missing in the bathroom that were critical to success. Make sure there is soap, a trashcan, Kleenex, and do I dare say tissue paper.

Make sure that not only is the house set up, but that distractions such as pets are minimized. For example, if there is a dog in the host home, it's generally best to put the dog somewhere other than where the group is meeting. Dogs, especially cute lap dogs, can be very disruptive to a group meeting. For the cat lovers reading this, your feline family member is also included in the same camp of disruptive capacity as a dog.

Here is a list logistical details you may want to consider as you prepare to host your small group:

- ☐ Extra Bibles
- ☐ Extra Pens/Pencils
- ☐ Lesson Materials
- ☐ Seating for everyone
- ☐ Kleenex

- ☐ Lights turned on
- ☐ Meeting room tidied
- ☐ Bathroom cleaned and supplied
- ☐ Name tags
- ☐ Porch light on if it is dark outside
- ☐ Room thermostat adjusted
- ☐ Pets isolated
- ☐ Time and location of future meetings
- ☐ Refreshments
- ☐ Childcare area prepared with snacks, toys, activities, wipes, first aid kit (and duct tape . . . just kidding).

Welcome small group members when they arrive. Don't panic if the response is small; just enjoy the fruit of the efforts you put into inviting others to your group. Sometimes the response may be small, but the key is persistency. After a couple of meetings, evaluate how things are going with your group to see if adjustments need to be made. Here's what a simple evaluation looks like: 1) What went well? 2) What could we do better or differently?

Key Phrase to Remember:

Develop a plan for your small group launch.

For Discussion

1. Share an experience of starting something new and the steps you took to start it.

2. What might be additional steps to starting a small group and maintaining momentum once it's begins?

3. What steps could you take if starting a new group misfires?

Chapter 3
It's All About Relationships

SECRET #2

"Without Building Relationships, The Bible Study Always Fall Short."

The beginning point for starting and leading a small group doesn't begin with the curriculum or the capacity of the host's home to hold a large number of people. The beginning point is to develop a relational environment on which trust can be fostered. The end goal of fostering trust is that you have a small group that allows God to move in and change lives.

What is a relational environment? Let's consider first what a relational environment is not. It is not sitting in rows listening to one person carrying the weight of the conversation or even lecturing disguised as teaching. A relational environment is not being inflexible in regards to the group's meeting agenda. Nor is a relational environment merely an exchange of knowledge. So, just to say you have a small group and therefore, also a relational environment is just not necessarily true.

Let's look at what makes a relational environment. It involves both the physical environment and the emotional openness towards one another including openness towards God. Both aspects need to be present in order for a relational environment to be present. The physical space should foster relationships and not hinder them. Having group members face each other is a great beginning to encourage such an environment. A relational environment is highly participatory. The goal of the leader is to foster conversation and collaboration. The leader works at inviting vulnerability and transparency. Fostering this type of relational environment makes up one of the most important foundational basics of a small group.

Vince Lombardi introduced the basics to his team by saying, "This is a football." In saying this, he was declaring the most important basic of the game. Similarly, God declares what is the most important basic of our faith when we give our lives to Him: "It's all about relationships." It's about a relationship with His son, Jesus Christ, and a relationship with those who follow Him. A small group isn't about a meeting; it's about those two relationships.

You may be thinking, "Relationships, . . . got it. I have them, enjoy them, and couldn't live without them."

However, the stark reality is that just because you get a group of people together, it doesn't mean that this group would ever experience community like the early church experienced (Acts 2:42-47). The early church expressed their love for one another by sharing unselfishly, spending time together building each other up, praying together for each other's needs, and studying what scripture was teaching them. There was an ingredient that provided the fuel for their relationships. It's the same ingredient we need to fuel our relationships. Without this one ingredient or quality, a small group can't and won't grow. That ingredient is trust. Without trust, you won't have a small group because no one will come to a meeting where there is fear of not being liked or disappointed. Every good relationship is grounded on trust.

So, how do you build trust? Trust begins with the small group leader. If I can't trust the small group leader and group members, I won't go to that small group. In order to build trust and create an environment where relationships can thrive, there are some behaviors that are required from the leader and group as a whole.

Here is a short list use can use with your small group to help guide conversation with each other. Before each study or discussion, read aloud each one of these guidelines with your group. Reading through them each time may sound crazy, but they work to create an understanding of how to communicate in ways that foster trust. Over time you will notice a tremendous payoff in the quality of relationships established.

Be revealing. Acquaintances don't experience much trust between each other; however, close friends do. The only way a relationship goes from acquaintanceship to a close friendship is when there is a mutual willingness to be known by one another. To be known requires transparency. Transparency can only grow when one risks being hurt by revealing oneself to the group. The depth of transparency will continue to grow as the risks of being hurt continue to be taken as self-revelation takes place within the group. There is no substitute when trying to build relationships than being self-revealing.

No fixing. Nothing drives me crazier in a small group than members in the group trying to fix someone else's problem. It's usually one of two extremes. They try to fix the problem by spiritualizing it by saying, "You just need to pray more," "God has a plan," or "You need to have more faith." While praying or having more faith is always a good thing, none of those alone fixes the problem. The other extreme is giving bad advice. It's not just advice, it's downright rotten advice. I still remember the advice one group member gave to another group member in regards to a sour business venture with another follower of Christ: "I think you should sue their socks off." Sarcastically speaking, that advice works well, especially when non-Christians see how two followers of Jesus treat one another.

There's one more reason not to fix someone else's problems. Most of the time, they aren't asking you to fix their problems. They simply want someone to know about the problem and to empathize with them in their plight. What happens most of the time when a group member gives advice, the person sharing shuts down and stops talking altogether.

No cross-talking. Cross-talk can be defined as a second conversation taking place while an initial conversation continues. When this takes place, group members end up talking over one another and nothing productive for the group happens. Cross-talking is the perfect way to make someone feel unimportant. Not only does it make people feel insignificant; it is just plain rude and disruptive. This type of behavior communicates to the rest of the group that the cross-talkers are a step above the rest and the rules about participation and respect don't apply to them.

No rescuing. Have you ever heard someone talking and have a difficult time getting the words out about embarrassing or awkward situation, and then, someone interrupts and finishes that person's thought or tries to make the other person feel better about their situation? That's rescuing. The best thing for the person who has a difficult time getting the words out is to let him struggle. He needs to struggle so he can be ready to share it again or to get a better handle on how to describe what happened. Also, when the listener decides to finish the other person's sentence, the person talking tends to feel like his story has been hijacked and doesn't continue to share. For all practical purposes, he has been shut down.

Use "I" statements. Taking ownership with one's words is difficult for some. They say things like "we feel" or "the church thinks" when in reality it is only how they feel. I have been in groups where group members would only use plural pronouns. In doing so, they would be including me and assume I felt the same as they did. That became very frustrating for me because I would have to go back around and say that it wasn't necessarily how the group felt. Group members rarely speak for the group unless they clarify that it is what they are hearing from the group. When group members speak using a plural pronoun, they are usually saying how they alone feel. When they use a plural pronoun, there is a tendency for them to distance themselves from their own words. Distancing oneself from one's own words doesn't lend itself to transparency, ownership, and an openness to change.

Maintain confidentiality. Life-changing relationships take time, but breaking confidentiality will ruin those same relationships in seconds. Confidentiality is one of the main ingredients to trust. Therefore, never assume no matter how benign or insignificant something shared seems to you, it always has greater importance and significance to the one who shared it. I remember sharing a simple prayer request with a small group I was leading. It was a very benign request for guidance in preparation for a presentation I had to give. It really didn't matter that anyone else outside the group knew. However, we had agreed as a group that all prayer requests would remain confidential. Yet, one of the ladies in my group shared it with another group as a well-intentioned prayer request.

When I found out, I was disappointed in her. Had she asked if she could share my request with others, I would have said, "Certainly." But, she didn't and my trust in her was not just in doubt, it was gone. The lesson of maintaining confidentiality is important because in reality, when it comes to someone else's story, it's really only theirs alone to share.

These six guidelines may seem obvious or perhaps common sense, but don't assume everyone knows how to interact in ways that foster relationships. Use these guidelines faithfully to build trusting relationships in your group.

Key Phrase to Remember:

Create an environment of trust.

For Discussion

1. Which of the guidelines that help build trust is easiest for you to do? The hardest?

2. How long do you think it takes to build trust in relationships? Why?

3. From your experience, what are other factors important to building trusting relationships?

Chapter 4

Welcoming with Acceptance

SECRET #3

"Here I Am!" or "There You Are!"

Kathy had a tough week. She had to work long hours in order to please her boss while still doing her best to take care of her family which also came with its own set of stresses. She wanted to go to her small group because she desperately wanted a break from that week's pressures. Wearily, she trudged through the host home's front door and was immediately greeted from the host with a "Have we met?" The host didn't mean harm, but Kathy wasn't in the mood to discern if the host was serious or not. He stepped on Kathy's last nerve. She just wanted a place she could feel a genuine welcome and be affirmed. She decided to stay at the group meeting that night, but she also decided to stay away from the host. That was the last time Kathy went to that small group.

Now, Kathy should have approached the host after she had calmed down that night to let him know about her hurt and her need for support. But, this wasn't the first time gentle hospitality had not been shown to her by the host. She had decided that was to be the final night she would attend. Based on Kathy's experience, I learned that the host cannot be merely friendly. I learned it's important to know how to be a friendly host who doesn't irritate the group members coming into the host's home.

Every time your small group meets, there is always a little trust, closeness, and acceptance that has leaked between group members because they haven't seen one another in a week. When you think about it, there are 2 hours a week spent in your group meeting and 166 hours living life outside that group time. One hundred sixty-six hours is a lot of time for life impacting moments to be experienced. This means that the same group members who attended your small group last week will not be the same people who will attend your small group this week. Therefore, it's important as a host to think strategically of how you can reduce people's fears and anxieties as they enter your home and welcome them with acceptance.

Reducing Group Members' Fears

The first thing to reduce fears and anxieties is to put on your best social graces. Don't try any funny business.

Simply be as polite as possible. Phrases like, "Howdy, stranger," or "What did you bring me?" tend to not be as funny nor as polite as one might think. A great rule of thumb is just to be as polite as possible. Saying phrases like, "It's so good to see you!" and "I am so glad you are here!" work much better than trying to be funny.

Let me put this in practical terms so that it is memorable. There are only two ways to greet people. You can great them with a "Here I am!" or a "There you are!" The "Here I am" is the trying to be clever and funny. The "Here I am" puts the attention on you rather than the group member coming into the host home. A "There you are!" is a much more welcoming approach. It sounds like, "It is so good to see you," or "How are you?"

Second, there are logistical matters that will help reduce their fears. Create a short checklist of things you can do to reduce group member's fears even before they get to the group. There is a slightly longer checklist in chapter 2. A short list is given here as a reminder of the impact logistical issues can have on a small group and that can help reduce a group member's fears:

- ☐ The porch light is turned on if it is dark outside.
- ☐ Name tags – don't under estimate the power of being able to call someone by name.
- ☐ Turn on enough lights so group members can easily read the small print in their Bibles.

☐ Turn on the hall and bathroom lights. These work like beacons directing the group members to the various rooms of necessity.

☐ Be aware of the thermostat and room temperature. The more bodies in a room, the more the room will heat up.

☐ Have plenty of supplies on hand including pencils and paper.

☐ Coffee, water, tea, or soda and any snacks are set up before group members arrive.

☐ Pets are put up. Even a small Chihuahua can unnerve your best group member.

☐ Set the chairs up in a circle. This set-up works much better than rows because no one will be looking at the back of someone else's head!

Host for Success in Every Activity

No matter what activity your group is doing, make sure everyone can participate and be successful in that activity. Nothing could be more deflating than not being able to participate with the rest of the small group in an activity. If you are doing Bible study, be sure to have extra Bibles or study notes. If you are certain that not everybody knows everyone's name, bring out the name tags. You may get grief for using them, but it communicates that you expect new people and that you aren't assuming everyone knows everyone else's name. A unique but increasingly more common issue are people's allergies. Some are allergic to scented candles, some to gluten, others to pets, and the list goes on. Hopefully, no one in your group is allergic to other group members. Err on the side of caution until you get to know your group members well enough to know if they have any specific allergies.

Welcoming with acceptance is more than a greeting. It has to do with every word spoken during the time a group member is present and includes all the logistics and supplies of every group meeting. The result is the same for both long term and new group members: people who are more likely to be open and prepared for change.

Key Phrase to Remember:

Welcome with Acceptance.

For Discussion

1. What do you think are the most important qualities of a small group host? (The kind and quality of snacks and food cannot be one of the answers.)

2. Do you tend to greet people with a "Here I am" or a "There you are"? Share why you think so.

3. How do you think a good host can impact the growth of the group members?

Chapter 5

The Group Covenant

SECRET #4

"Every Group Has A Covenant, Make Sure Yours Is Written."

Gary was frustrated, one might say even angry, with his small group because they consistently failed to do their homework in preparation for their study. Gary called me one evening in desperation saying that he was stepping down as the leader of his small group because he had failed to help his group grow spiritually. He said that they didn't seem to take their Bible study seriously, and that they never did their homework. Gary felt he had failed his group. He was convinced they didn't want to grow and that he was not able to motivate and inspire them to capture the desire to grow. Only after a conversation took place between Gary and his small group did the group realize the intense feelings Gary had about their lack of doing homework. However, this realization didn't convince them to change their minds and agree to do homework before their group meetings. It wasn't that Gary had an inflexible small group, they just didn't feel they could make the commitment to complete homework every week.

For the first time, Gary discovered the truth that no matter how much inspiration he gave to his small group, they would never do homework in preparation for their small group meeting. Gary thought he could simply tell his small group what he expected them to do. He didn't realize they would have to own homework as a value which they would practice. Instead, they held the value that they wouldn't do homework because they didn't have time for homework. They all had full-time jobs, most were parents with more than one child, there were sports team commitments that required the parents take the kids to and from practices and games, and the group members also had responsibilities of serving in other church ministries. As we continued to process Gary's dilemma, it became apparent that he and his small group had not taken the time to agree on a set of values commonly known as a group covenant or group agreement.

The Role of the Covenant

After that night's discussion about homework, Gary continued to lead his small group. Gary and his group also talked through how they would work and communicate with each other as a group. Amazingly, I was able to witness a cloud of confusion and discord be lifted after their conversation. The reality is simple: Every small group has its own unique way in which its group members interact and relate with one another. Sometimes this interaction is healthy, sometimes it's hurtful. Whether this interaction is good or bad, it is motivated by each group member's own understanding of how a group is supposed to behave. This understanding of how group members are to behave fall into a category one would call expectations. Just as Gary and his small group members had their own individual expectations, you and I also have our own expectations. And our expectations are what we covenant ourselves to give to someone else or a group of people. Those expectations form the ground rules for your small group. Even if you don't have a covenant that is written, you still have a covenant because every group member brings their own understanding of what the expectations should be for the group. Therefore, if it's not written, you have as many covenants as you do people in your small group. It becomes only a matter of time before some kind of conflict happens within the group.

The covenant's role is to help group members come to the same understanding of how their small group will function. The covenant acts like a school playground fence that is there to protect children from all kinds of hazards. Every good school playground has a fence lining its boarders. Without the fence, the children who use the playground run the risk of going beyond the boundary of its safety. If they go beyond the fence, there is the danger of being hurt. At my school's playground, I knew when a soccer ball was kicked over the fence that I needed my teacher to go outside the fence or to give me permission to recover the ball so that my risk of being hurt was less. The group covenant is like the playground fence. It will help your group build trust and get the most out of the group experience, just as a fence does with the safety of a playground. When the group needs to go outside it's boundary, the group leader, like the teacher, needs to step in to guide the group.

What's In a Covenant?

Every good small group covenant has three parts. Just as a stool has three legs in order to stand, the covenant also has three legs on which the group stands. If one leg is missing, the covenant won't be able to provide the guidance and ground rules your small group needs to thrive.

The first leg of the covenant is the purpose. This is the most important element of the covenant because it gives your group the reason for being. Groups that aim at nothing not only hit nothing, they may end up hitting each other. Does your small group exist for Bible study? For fellowship? Does your group exist to shepherd and care for those in your group? Does it exist to be an extension of the church and help accomplish its mission? My small group's purpose is three-fold: To connect with one another, change to be more like Jesus Christ, and to cultivate a heart for serving others. Because this three-fold purpose is fairly vague, we have talked about what each part of the purpose means and have put specifics to it. I have met more than one person who has been frustrated because the small group was not doing what he thought it was supposed to do. Some would say, "All my small group does is eat; I want to do Bible study." Or I hear, "All my group does is watch movies and doesn't study the Bible." As it turned out the movies that were being watched were DVD-driven small group Bible studies. While every group in your church may have the same purpose, each group will express it differently and uniquely.

The second leg of the covenant is the guidelines. The guidelines give you and your small group structure to your meetings. The guidelines answer what time your meeting starts and what time it ends. It also answers who's going to do what. Will group members share the responsibility of bringing snacks or will the host provide them? What kinds of foods are acceptable? Decide how you will address childcare. Discuss each of the below guidelines with your group.

We agree to the following expectations:
- This group will normally meet every:

- Actual meeting time is to begin at:
  and end at:

- We will meet at:

- Refreshments or meals will be handled in the following manner:

- Childcare will be handled in the following manner:

Don't take any of these guidelines for granted because they provide the skeleton on which the muscles of the group hang. The muscles of your small group make up the third leg of your covenant.

The third leg of the covenant is the things the group will value. Values define how your small group will interact with each other. These values will assist with group conflict and provide guidance at various times through the life of your small group. If your group says that confidentiality is important, then your small group members shouldn't share with other people things that are shared in the small group no matter how insignificant it seems to be. Here is a list of some of the items a small group may value.

We agree to the following values:
- **Confidentiality.** We agree that anything that is shared in our small group, stays in our small group whether it was shared as a prayer request or in our discussion.

- **Priority.** We agree to give priority to the small group meetings and not let other activities interfere with it. If I am running late, I will let someone in our group know we are on our way.

- **Participation.** We agree to encourage others to engage in discussions and group life. I will be participate in a way that allows for others to equally participate.

- **Accessibility.** We agree to give each other permission to contact each other, even in the middle of the night if needed.

- **Openness.** We seek to be honest and transparent with one another and agree not to fix one another in the process.

- **Respect.** We agree to communicate with one another in ways that are respectful and give advice only when it's requested. We also agree that we can only confess our sins and not someone else's sin.

- **Open Chair.** We agree to keep an empty chair for others who are not a part of the group, but need a group as we do for spiritual growth and care. The open chair is not for Jesus. He is already present and doesn't need a chair.

Take time to talk with your group about each value. Ask a few questions about each value. For example, the first value in our covenant you could ask one or more of the questions below:

Confidentiality. We agree that anything that is shared in our small group, stays in our small group whether it was shared as a prayer request or in our discussion.

1. What is your expectation about our agreement for confidentiality?

2. When do you think it is okay to share something said in the group to someone outside the group?

3. Is it okay for you to share outside the group something you shared in the group?

Golden Rules for Using a Covenant

I have a few Golden Rules for using a small group covenant so that the covenant does what it is intended to do. First, every group, no matter the size or purpose, needs to have a written covenant. It's my experience that most problems small groups experience can be solved if they have a covenant or if they would follow their covenant. While a covenant won't prevent conflict or confusion among group members, it is a great tool in navigating group issues.

Second, the covenant exists to serve your group. Your small group does not serve your covenant. I have seen some groups struggle because they get caught in the trap of being a slave to their covenant. Mike led a group that understood the value of a covenant and faithfully followed it; however, they had a struggle created by their covenant. Mike's group was large and the house that hosted their small group was out of room to add new people. They continued, though, to practice the value of the open chair. As Mike's small group pastor, I had emphasized in training the importance of using a covenant, but I had failed to instruct him on when the covenant needs to change as the group changes. Mike's group was getting very stressed because of their desire to follow their covenant. In fact they were feeling guilty because they could no longer have an open chair. Once Mike discovered he could change the covenant's values, he and his group took the open chair value out and replaced it with a focus on raising up another leader who could begin a new group.

How to Create a Covenant

I love when a small group creates its own covenant from scratch. I believe that creating your own covenant rather than using a pre-written one increases the ownership that group members feel towards their group. It also builds trust as relationships within the group are formed, and as mentioned before, trust is the foundation that allows an openness for growth.

There are just a few steps in building your own small group covenant. First, plan to devote one of your first group meetings to discuss the two questions below and have a white board on which someone is recording everyone's responses. I have found that a flip chart with a sticky back works well. The first question to ask is, "What do hope to gain by being a part of this small group?" The responses you get will vary from friendship, spiritual growth, and support to name a few. Once you believe the group is ready to move on to the next question, ask, "What is a fear you have about being a part of this group?" Again, your group's responses will vary and could include: group members sharing my secrets, people forming cliques and leaving me out, and not being able to meet a group member's expectations.

Next, take the responses and place each response on a separate sheet of paper or sticky note. Place them on a table or on the wall and ask for everyone in the small group to take a turn and place them in like categories. As this part of the process takes place, the group members will probably realign the categories. When the last person has arranged the responses in larger categories, label each category. Then assign everyone in the group one of the categories and ask them to write a statement that explains the shared values important to the small group. After the process is complete, you not only have shared values, but you have also created increased ownership, unity, and trust in your small group.

In my current small group, we did this process as I explained above. By doing this process, our small group experienced unity and togetherness because we made it our own instead of what someone else said should be our covenant. What follows are the final results as to our small group's values as they are expressed in our covenant:

Values

Community. We all like close community. We will strive to have fun together inside and outside of LifeGroup to build friendships with each other.

Trust. We all fear letting our guard down for fear of being hurt due to our imperfect nature. In this group, we will trust each other, keep things in confidence and strive not to judge each other.

Commitment to Growth. We desire to grow in our Christian walk and realize that this growth best happens in purposeful community. We will encourage each other to express our different perspectives through study and conversation to spur one another towards that growth.

Uplifting Relationships. We agree to lift each other up by encouraging one another with our words and praying for one another.

Transparent Accountability. We commit to be transparent with one another and to hold each other accountable.

Every small group covenant can and may look different from other covenants. The important thing is that your group knows and understands their own group covenant. If you need an example to get started writing your own group covenant, there is a sample group covenant in the appendices of this book. Use it in formatting your own or use it and make it better! Then after the completion of a multi-week study, grab the covenant and walk through it again with your group members. As you do, talk about each point of the covenant asking how the group as a whole is achieving it and making adjustments to it as you go.

Key Phrase to Remember:

Use a covenant.

For Discussion

1. How do you feel when your expectations are not met?

2. Have you ever been a part of a small group that used a covenant? If so, did the covenant contribute anything to the group? If not, what difference might it have made? Explain.

3. In your opinion, what are non-negotiable items to have in a small group covenant?

Chapter 6

Facilitating A Small Group

SECRET #5

"Don't Think Airliner When Leading, Think White Water Rafting."

Of all the small group meetings I have attended, I can remember the details of only about ten of them. The one I remember most wasn't a pleasant meeting. In fact, it was very painful. It wasn't that there was conflict, rather it was how the small group meeting was being facilitated. When it came time for the lesson, the leader took out the book on which our study was based and read two full pages. He didn't skip a paragraph. Did I mention that he alone read the pages to the group? We knew he was done reading when he woke us up with a question about what he had read. He asked us, "How did this section impact you?" While we considered how we were impacted, he began to answer his own question. Once he was done answering his own question, he did what a good leader would do. He asked a follow-up question, "Who else has anything to add?" The truth was that in answering his own question, he didn't leave the rest of us much to add, so we didn't. This pattern was repeated for the entire 45 minutes of our Bible study. I felt bad for the leader, but I felt worse for the rest of the group. While the leader was a devoted and mature follower of Jesus, he didn't understand the principle of facilitating a small group that works.

The Secret to a Great Group Isn't Your Teaching Ability

I like the way my friend, Jake Zauche, describes the best approach to facilitating a group that produces life-change. He says, "Don't think airliner when leading a small group." In an airplane the pilot sits in the cockpit, separate from the rest of the passengers and crew. Other than the flight crew, the pilot does everything to get the passengers to their destination. The pilot is the one who operates the controls to make the plane take off and land, so the passengers don't have any responsibility for getting to their destination. They only have to sit, sip their soda, take a nap, or read and wait for the pilot to get them to their destination safely.

Likewise, a small group leader shouldn't try to be like the pilot of an airplane. This type of leader does everything for the small group and then some. For example, this leader leads the group by taking a book, even a very good book, and reading large sections aloud. After reading, he explains what he just read. When it comes to prayer time, he alone says the prayer out loud. For their social meetings, he plans what the group will do. The leader is acting as though he were the airline pilot. He does everything for the small group, so   the group is there only for the fellowship and can't fulfill its greater purpose.

Think White Water Rafting!

A good small group leader thinks white water rafting. Riding down the rapids, there is a guide who sits in the back of the raft with his eyes on the river ahead and on his passengers who aren't just sitting and sipping soda. They have been equipped with oars to help move the raft safely forward. Everybody works together; however, it's the guide who is giving directions leading the group down the river. The guide isn't the one who physically has total control over the direction of the raft, but he does give directions to each person as he deems necessary to get the raft safely through the rapids.

A good small group leader is the guide rather than the teacher or authority. The goal is group participation. A good rule of thumb so the facilitator can intentionally plan and participate is the 80/20 rule. As a leader, you allow yourself to talk twenty percent of the time so that rest of the group can talk eighty percent. Implementing the 80/20 rule dictates that the leader asks good questions in order to facilitate discussion. When there is good group discussion about scripture and its application, then there is an opening for the Holy Spirit to come into the group to change lives.

Putting The Pieces Together

The small group that changes lives doesn't take a leader who is the cleverest, the most creative, or even the most brilliant. It does, however, take a leader who will lead the group as the guide. A group won't experience life-change unless someone is leading this process that brings about that change. It takes a leader who understands who he is and how God has created him. It also takes a leader who understands and practices his role as the guide. It's then that the small group leader is prepared to change the world.

Key Phrase to Remember:

Think White-Water Raft Guide.

For Discussion

1. In your own words describe the difference between the small group leader who acts like a pilot and the leader who acts like a white-water raft guide.

2. In what other relationships does this type of leadership work well?

3. What do you think might be limitations of leading from the perspective of the white-water raft guide?

Chapter 7

Asking Good Questions

SECRET #6

"Life- Change Isn't Forced, It's Facilitated."

I don't remember where I first heard the phrase, but it has proven true over and over again. It's a phrase that helps explain how people grow and in the case of leading a small group Bible study it explains how people grow spiritually. The phrase that has become an axiom in my life is this: "Life-change happens best when people discover Biblical truth for themselves."

I have to be honest; every time I share this phrase I feel a little guilty. Even though I believe it's true, I feel like I am betraying our preacher. Our preacher prepares a message every week and I feel I am saying that small groups are better than his sermon. The preacher tells us Biblical truth in compelling ways, but small groups allow for discussion and self-discovery of Biblical truth. The truth is that you and I need both teaching from the weekly message and the opportunity to discuss and live out scripture in the context of supportive relationships. When push comes to shove, however, small groups win over sermons. The reason small group discussion is best is that people have more ownership in what they learn than if they simply sit and listen to someone teaching. For that reason we call our small group leaders "facilitators" instead of "teachers."

What I Learned By Playing With Legos

When I train new small group leaders, I like to use an activity called the Lego Exercise. I divide my training group up into teams of 3 to 5 people, then equally divide up a container of Legos, and give them these instructions: Build something – anything you want, but everyone has to participate by connecting Lego pieces to their creation, and it must have at least one moving part. After about 15 minutes, I bring the groups together and ask them to share with the other groups what they've made.

After they've shared, I move to part two of the exercise in which I instruct them what to make out of the Legos. Everyone in the group takes turns, I don't tell them what they are making (it really doesn't matter anyway because it's generally nothing in particular). No one is allowed to help anyone else. If someone doesn't put the pieces together the way I want, I scold them. Generally speaking, I make this part of the exercise uncomfortable and stressful. After a few minutes I stop the activity. We then talk about what everyone experienced. I begin asking, "If I were to ask you to tear apart your creation or my creation, which would you tear apart first." Ten out of ten times, they respond with a resounding, "Yours!" We then talk about why they responded that way. First, they hated the way I led them because I was acting as a teacher who didn't tell them what they were making and if they didn't go the direction I wanted, I would talk down to them. Second, they had a good time building their own creation. Finally, someone will say, "I prefer the thing I made because I built it, I have ownership in it. It's mine, not yours." You can see where this activity is taking us. It takes us right back to "Life-change happens best when people discover Biblical truth for themselves." It takes a facilitator to lead them on this journey of discovery which means that he leads as a raft guide instead of an airline pilot. Therefore, great facilitators ask good, well thought through questions.

The Tools of The Small Group Leader

Questions are to a small group as sermons are to a worship service. Questions are the tools of the small group leader. Let's take a look at questions, what types of questions exist and what is their function in the discussion process. The progression of the Bible study discussion is all about understanding the process people take as they discover truth for themselves. The process of how people change through discussion questions looks like this:

1. The topic is introduced through an **opening question** which helps the group member start thinking about the topic.
2. Then, the facts of the topic in the Bible passage are clarified through **observation questions**.
3. The topic is further clarified through **interpretation questions** which hopefully brings about an "Ah, ha" moment.
4. Finally the topic with its "Ah,ha" idea is specifically or measurably applied through **application questions**.

I want to remove the mystery of when and how to use each question. When God created the universe He also created only four types of questions. Just as there are a definitive number of chemical elements on the periodic table, there are only four types of questions in the entire universe. Understanding how to use these questions effectively will not only help you prepare lessons that change lives, but you will also be able to adjust those questions. You will also be able to confidently include new questions to help take your group to your planned destination.

Opening Questions

Opening questions help your group members begin to think about the topic you are getting ready to study. These questions should be worded so that everyone in your group can answer and then, with more than a "yes" or "no" answer. Here are a few examples of good and bad opening questions:

Topic	Bad Opening Questions
• Spiritual Gifts	How many spiritual gifts can you name?
• Priorities	Do you have enough time to get everything done at work?
• Possessions	What did you experience when you bought your first new car?
• Community	What is the name of a good childhood friend?

These are bad questions because they don't allow for more than a yes or no answer, ask about experiences group members may never have had, or are questions that don't convey significance. Let's look at a revision of the questions.

Topic	Good Opening Questions
• Spiritual Gifts	What is a memorable gift you received and what made it special?
• Priorities	Looking at your calendar, what things take up most of your time?
• Possessions	What is something you would find hard to give up and what would it require to give up?
• Community	What is the name of a memorable childhood friend and what made that person special?

Opening questions also serve a purpose beyond connecting with the topic. They also help your group members reconnect with one another. As I previously mentioned, there are one hundred sixty eight hours in a week. If your small group meets for two hours, that means your group has experienced one hundred sixty six hours of living since your last group meeting. A lot can happen in those hours. If your group members are not in touch with each other during meetings, trust has to be rebuilt. Without trust, your group is less likely to share anything of importance as you facilitate the discussion. Utilize the opening question to rebuild trust before you get to more personally revealing questions.

Observation Questions

Observation questions follow the reading of the scripture text and help group members discover the facts of the passage. In other words, these questions help you find the who, what, when, and where of the text. Ask observation questions that will help your group members connect with the lesson's theme rather than asking as many questions as you can. Usually two or maybe three observation questions are enough to help set the scene for the lesson's theme.

Examples of Observation Questions

- What did Jesus say?
- Who did Jesus say it to?
- How did those who heard Jesus respond?

Interpretation Questions

Once the context of the scripture and topic is established, move to the interpretation questions to uncover motivations of the people in the Bible story. These questions uncover the why and how. An interesting shift takes place between the observation and interpretation questions. They shift from telling the Bible story through the observation questions to telling the group member's story through the interpretation questions. The interpretation questions help each group member put themselves into the Bible story by sharing what the Bible characters must have experienced and felt.

Examples of Interpretation Questions

- How would you have responded to Jesus' words?
- What is challenging about Jesus' words?
- Share why you are encouraged or discouraged by what Jesus said.

Application Questions

Once the group member has put himself into the Bible story, move to the application questions that give your group members the chance to take the truths learned and discover how to apply them in practical ways individually and as a group. Good application questions always expect specific and measurable responses. They are never vague or theoretical. These questions ask for specific action. Not only do application questions look at how one will individually implement the truth learned, but also how application can be group action as well.

Examples of Application Questions

- What is Jesus asking you to do?
- What will you do to increase your commitment to Jesus this week?
- How are we as a group specifically going to make a difference?

Small Group Lesson Sample

Here's what it looks like when you put the four types of questions together in one lesson. We'll explore the story in Matthew 19 about the Rich Young Man. To determine the direction the questions will lead we'll pick *idolatry* as the lesson's theme. As you read and study through the questions, notice the subtle shift of the questions asking group members to retell the Bible story, to the group members putting themselves in the Bible story, to group members applying scripture as they tell their own story.

OPENING QUESTION
1. Besides family, what do people often treat as their favorite possession?

Ask a volunteer to read Matthew 19:16 – 24.

OBSERVING SCRIPTURE
2. What did the young man ask Jesus?

3. How did Jesus reply?

INTERPRETING SCRIPTURE
4. Why do you think the young man asked his question?

5. Why do you think Jesus omitted the commands to love God and added the command to sell all he had and give it to the poor?

APPLYING SCRIPTURE

6. What are some things in your life that you would have the hardest time giving up? Why?

7. What is Jesus asking you to give up in order to have a closer relationship with Him?

You can see how simple the questions can be to create a lesson that allows one to open up and let God enter the process of conforming us into the image of Christ. It simply takes knowing how to use the right type of question at the right time. Like anything new, it takes time and practice to become comfortable with this simple process through which God designed us to learn best.

Understanding the four types of questions and how they compliment and build on each other will give you the ability to customize Bible study lessons you have purchased. You will be able to understand the flow of the lesson and the direction towards which the questions are guiding your small group. Once you see how the author constructed each lesson, you have the ability to make smart adjustments by adding, removing, or changing questions in order to make the lesson most effective for your small group. And, your confidence as a facilitator of your group's Bible lesson will grow.

Key Phrase to Remember:

Ask Good Questions.

For Discussion

1. Do you believe in the phrase "Life-change happens when people discover biblical truth for themselves"? Why or why not?

2. What might be some limitations of the above phrase?

3. Which one of the four types of questions do you believe is indispensable for a small group lesson?

Chapter 8

Practicing Accountability

SECRET #7

"Lives Are Not Changed By How Much You Know, But By How Accountable You Are."

Can I just say that accountability scares me. When I think of someone holding me accountable, I usually picture someone of who has power over me because they now know my inner secrets that I have hidden. I also imagine the worse case scenario about this person; that he is heavy handed and lacking any grace. In fact, I picture a person who thrills at the idea of catching me doing something wrong. Or I imagine myself answering a series of accountability questions in a way where I skirt the truth. This keeps me off the hook so the other person doesn't think any less of me than what I know is the reality about myself. For years, I thought accountability was only for the brave at heart. In reality, accountability doesn't have to be something to fear. It doesn't have to be anything I pictured in my description above. However, it does have to be built around truth and grace that is always active and never passive. With the qualities of truth and grace being practiced within an accountability relationship, I believe that God does his best work. Without both, accountability can become either legalistic or weak. We'll unpack in a moment how truth and grace work together in an accountability relationship.

When you practice accountability with your small group, I think it's important for your small group to define what accountability looks like for them because accountability comes in different levels of intensity. The matter of fact is that a group's accountability will only be superficial if that small group has not spent time together. Spending time developing an understanding of what an accountability relationship looks like will bring about a common understanding of accountability. It will also build trust in relationships between those who are accountability partners.

Let's look at what life-changing accountability can do. Life-changing, rather than guilt laying, accountability consists of two qualities: truth and grace. You can't have life-changing accountability through either of them alone. Truth is defined as what we know from scripture as God's will for our lives. Grace is providing an avenue through which one person assists another in changing habits or achieving something good. I have experienced ineffective accountability relationships that only involved affirming the truth about my inadequacy to do the right thing and in return offered only a passive grace declaring God will forgive that sin. The normal result was that I was still left to overcome the sin on my own strength, but in addition, now I could also be embarrassed about it as I shared it with my "accountability partner."

It has been my experience that my life hasn't changed because I learned something new. I have discovered that life-change has always happened when I learned something new and then practiced it until it became a habit. I discovered that I practiced my new habit best when someone else practiced it with me. When it became a habit, I knew that I owned that truth or virtue.

Practical Ways to Practice Accountability with Your Small Group

Let's talk about accountability within your small group. As you know, spiritual growth, or any growth for that matter, doesn't happen quickly. It takes time and happens when the right catalysts are in place. It's amazing how much growth happens when there is even just a little catalyst that can turn a person in a new direction. As it only takes a slight movement of the steering wheel in a car to make a significant turn, it only takes small adjustments to make significant changes in one's life.

A small group that practices accountability requires someone who will lead and model the process. The simplest way to keep your small group members accountable is to utilize accountability during the small group meeting. As a regular habit with your Bible study, follow-up each week on what the group applied in last week's Bible study. I remember the night a friend led our small group. He didn't start the lesson the way he was "supposed to" according to our printed study guide. He started by asking, "Let's take a moment to share how our projects went last week as our response to the application question." I immediately realized I had done nothing. Then, I thought "I am probably in good company" and that few others did anything as well. I was wrong.

As we went around the circle, one by one, every group member had a story to tell about their project. I was the lone group member who had nothing to share. That was the last time I went to my small group unprepared to answer for last week's application question.

It takes at least two people to create accountability. Let's say I have a problem with being physically out of shape. My doctor insists that I exercise or run the risk of damaging my body or worse: death. However, I don't exercise in spite of knowing that my health depends on it. The best time I have available is in the early morning hours. I share my intent with my group, but I have a very hard time disciplining myself to get up in the morning to workout.

Suppose one of my friends in our small group is aware of my issue. He says, "Why don't I help you be accountable for exercising? I will come by your house at

6:00 a.m. three mornings a week and I will take you to the gym and we will work out together." He follows through with his commitment and in the course of a few weeks, I now am awake and ready to be picked up before he arrives at my house. I also look forward to him picking me up because he has become an important friend and our relationship has been a great support to me personally. That's what good accountability looks like.

Accountability always requires action and not just words alone. The truth is that I need to get in physical shape and grace is extended to me when my friend helps me change by picking me up to work out together. My friend's grace is not passive. He doesn't tell me to go to bed earlier or have my wife wake me up. He doesn't offer any platitudes. He sacrifices his time and his energy to show me that he cares about me and wants me to get into better health. He has to give up something so he can serve my needs.

When you think about this type of accountability, it really isn't any different than the type of truth and grace that our Heavenly Father extends to us. The truth is that we have sinned and we need a savior. If the role of the savior were to say, "You're forgiven," or "don't do that again," would that be the grace that the consequences of sin demands? No. Sin demands a grace that is active rather than passive.

Our Heavenly Father sent His son, Jesus, to die in our place so that we could be forgiven of our sins. This wasn't a passive grace like the grace many experience in an accountability relationship where only words and platitudes are shared. It was very much a grace that took action as Jesus lived a perfect life and allowed himself to die in our place. This type of grace is life-changing and life-giving.

The type of grace God offers is the same kind of grace I want to extend. It is much better than the concept of grace that produces legalism and guilt.

Key Phrase to Remember:

Practice accountability.

For Discussion

1. In what relationships are you currently accountable to someone else? What is the purpose for this accountability?

2. What makes accountability life-giving? Oppressive?

3. When is it good for small group members to be accountable to one another? When is it not?

Chapter 9

Listening With Understanding

SECRET #8

"Transparency Requires More Than Talking, It Requires Listening."

I remember the night, the home, and the kitchen table where we were sitting. I had decided that for this small group meeting we would share our spiritual stories. I knew for it to be successful I would have to be first and in sharing my story I had to be real and transparent. I shared my story first. I thought I did well without getting too deep and we moved on to the next person at the table. She started to share and about 60 seconds into her story she said, "I have never shared this with anyone before . . . "and then began to unfold a secret that had changed her life and told of how God showed up. She finished and we affirmed her by saying, "Thanks for sharing." We moved to the next person. Sixty seconds into his story, he said, "I have never shared this with anyone before . . ." and then began to share his secret. When he finished, several of us simply said, "Thanks for sharing." As we continued around the table, several others shared stories they had hidden inside of them for many years. Every group member made the group a safe place to share hidden parts of their lives. They didn't try to fix the tragic stories so the person would feel better, they didn't share their own similar war story, nor did they have side conversations while each person shared. It was a night to appreciate where each of us had come from and how God helped us. It was a defining moment for our small group. That night we experienced what Biblical community looked like. To achieve this, all we did was listen.

What Listening Isn't

Too often, people think that they must talk in order to impact a life. The truth is, listening is just as powerful, but not everyone is good at listening. Even those who are good listeners still have to work hard to be effective listeners. Rather than focusing on what a good listener does, let's talk about what a good listener doesn't do.

First, good listeners don't talk. Good listeners know when to be quiet and when to talk. You can't listen when you talk. Good listeners don't tell their own "war story." As an example, someone tells something horrific and another person follows up by saying, "You think you had it bad, let me tell you about my experience . . . "

Good listeners don't try to fix another person's problem. This happens most of the time by giving advice. Giving advice is one of the worst things a group member can do. It's not that their advice may not be valuable; however, if the person didn't ask for it, he probably isn't ready to receive it. Or perhaps you have heard a group member express hurt over a neighbors actions and another group member says, "Rub some dirt on it and shake it off!" First of all, it's not the best advice. Second, the group member wanted the small group to just listen.

Good listeners also don't try to minimize another person's story. Again, in this case the listener is no longer the listener and becomes the talker. In the midst of a tragedy, a group member may say, "This tragedy is all a part of God's will and He will provide for you." In this case the group member has failed to recognize the impact of the story and has minimized its importance.

What is Listening with Understanding?

Good listening involves three simple components: A tentative opening, identifying feelings, and identifying content. Let's look at each part of being an active listener.

The tentative opening is just that: tentative. It lets the one talking know that you don't presume to know what he has felt and experienced. At the same time it also signals to the speaker that you have been trying to understand what they have just shared.

Here are a few examples of tentative openings:

- It sounds like . . .
- You seem to be . . .
- You appear to be . . .
- What I hear you say is . . .

As you read these examples you may think that these phrases sound like you are trying to move to a counseling mode where you turn your small group into a therapy or support group. In reality, however, an attempt to counsel isn't what the other person is thinking as you add the next two components. What they will hear with the tentative opening is someone who is trying to listen and understand.

The second component is identifying the feelings that the other person has identified in sharing. Examples of feelings that might be expressed are:

- Angry
- Happy
- Excited
- Frustrated
- Helpless
- Confused
- Stunned
- Amazed
- Proud

If a feeling is not verbalized, don't assume you know how he is feeling and therefore, don't say how he is feeling. If the talker says that he is feeling sad, don't use the word "unhappy" because he isn't unhappy, he is sad. The two words may be synonyms, but the word shared is the word he owns and understands. Reflecting that word back to him will communicate that you were listening and not that you are trying to reshape his story. The next component of active listening is identifying the content whether or not a feeling has been identified,

Identifying the content gives you the context of the statement or conversation. Again, as with identifying the feeling, identifying and reflecting back to the speaker what he has shared reinforces the fact that you are wanting to understand what he is sharing. Here are some examples of things people might share and we'll use to practice identifying the content:

- An old friend who unexpectedly called
- Being snowed in after a fierce snow storm
- Finding a $20 bill on the sidewalk
- Family member arrested
- Pet ran away
- Getting 10 hours of sleep last night
- Aging parents
- Stress at work
- Health issues

Here's what it looks like when you put all the three components together using examples of each component previously given:

- It sounds like you are excited that an old friend unexpectedly called you.
- You seem to be feeling happy because you got 10 hours of sleep last night.
- Finding a $20 bill on the sidewalk would make me happy, too.
- It seems that you are frustrated because you were snowed in after the fierce snow storm.
- How best to help aging parents can be confusing.

You probably noticed that that third example of putting the components together didn't include a tentative opening. This is to illustrate how conversations are not simply cut and dry because every conversation is unique and different. As the listener, a conversation doesn't always follow the format of a tentative open, identify the feeling, and identifying the content. At times, the listener may just give a head nod, an "I see," and often ask follow-up questions. Follow-up questions can help clarify what the person is experiencing and feeling. Based on the situation, such follow-up questions could include:

- "Tell me more about what happened."
- "Can you describe it to me?"
- "What did you do?"
- "What happened next?"
- "What was going through your mind?"

The key to being a good listener is to reflect back to those who are sharing the same words they use to identify feelings and content. A good listener never finishes another person's story. Rather, the listener works to pull out the other person's story through follow-up questions and being a good active listener.

Key Phrase to Remember:

Listen with understanding.

For Discussion

1. Take a few minutes to practice listening with others in your group using the three components of active listening.

2. As the listener, what did you do well? What could you have done better?

3. What was one of the most difficult things about being an active listener?

Chapter 10
Keeping The Group On Track

SECRET #9
___
"A Group on Track Gets to Its Destination."
___

Gary had been leading his group for about a year and a half when one of his first group members started the habit of arriving late. It wasn't just ten or fifteen minutes late. She consistently arrived an hour late for a two hour group meeting. Gary and a few other couples had become used to this behavior even though their group's covenant stated a specific start and end time. Gary's group had continued to grow and the group member continued to arrive very late. It wasn't just that she arrived late, it was that her arrival often interrupted the group study at a point the group was starting to be transparent with one another. Upon her late arrival the small group would pause the discussion to greet her and, therefore, disrupting the flow of the meeting. Any transparency and moment of openness was gone and had to be recaptured. The weight of the situation was a blind spot for Gary until one night when some of the newer group members shared its disruptive impact. The group could no longer put up with it. It was then that Gary finally realized the group member's extreme tardiness was derailing the group.

This could be any small group's story, but it doesn't have to be about a group member who is always late. It could be a group member who would rather talk about politics or sports or the latest department store sale. Any of these will get your small group off track and will not only frustrate other group members, but will be opportunities lost for life-changing moments.

Types of Disruptive Behavior

Let's look at some general behaviors that can cause your small group to be derailed and then look at some possible solutions to fix it. Note that these are not people types. These are only behaviors because at any point in our lives, you and I have the potential of displaying any one of these behaviors.

Negative Talk. The person who displays this behavior always sees at least one thing that isn't right with the world. It could revolve around church, politics, or something else that makes people uncomfortable to talk about. The person talks about it like an old vinyl record that is scratched and repeats itself over and over again.

The amazing thing is that regardless of what your small group discusses, the person with the negative speak behavior always finds a way to connect the study to their negative view. For example, Bob was a group member who had a cunning way of connecting our country's president to every impending judgment mentioned in the Bible. Then, there was Bonnie who mentioned weekly that she wished our senior pastor would preach the Bible. Regardless of the negative comments topic, the negative comments have a tendency to suck the life right out of the group. Therefore, it can't be ignored.

How do you get your group back on track when someone exhibits negative talk? First, don't try to fix it on the spot or try to explore the negative speak further in the middle of the group's discussion. As gently and as directly as you can say that it is a topic for another time or that it deserves another conversation at later time. Then, jump back into the topic you were discussing with your group before the negative comments occurred.

If this behavior becomes a regular practice and not just a passing negative comment, plan to talk to the group member outside the group meeting time. During this conversation, open up the conversation by saying, "It sounds like you feel strongly about _____. Can you help me understand?" You don't have to agree with the person's opinion; you only need to acknowledge that it's how that person feels. After the person has shared, thank him or her. If it is a matter that can be resolved by having a conversation with the person towards whom the negative comment is focused, ask the concerned group member to talk with the other person since that would be the right thing to do. If he refuses, then request that they no longer bring it up. If it is something out of their control, gently help that person be aware of how the comments come across to you and maybe some of the group. You aren't asking the person to change his opinion, just to be aware that not everyone feels the same way nor with the same intensity and that it takes the group off track.

Over-Talkative. The person who displays this behavior dominates the discussion and sometimes even the topic. The group feels not only helpless, but derailed in their pursuit of learning what the leader has prepared. The over-talkative person isn't the one who just needs to share because he has just had something exciting or possibly tragic happen. The over-talkative person is the who has the weekly pattern of talking more than anyone else in the group and is not always on topic. When I think of the over-talkative behavior, I usually think of Jesus' disciple, Peter. Peter was often the first to speak up and was definitely the outspoken person of the all the disciples. In fact, I picture Jesus having to take Peter aside from time to time to address Peter's over-talkative behavior.

How do you get your group back on track when you have been derailed by over-talkative behavior? There are all kinds of subtle hints that a leader can give such as sitting next to the person, asking for other people in the group to respond first, using a "talking stick" where only the person holding the stick can speak, or giving everyone only a certain amount of time to share a response. These are well-meaning and can be effective, but may not address the problem behavior.

The one way that works is for the leader to have a conversation with the over-talkative individual outside the group time. Begin by asking the over-talkative person how he thinks the group is going. As the conversation progresses, ask the other person for permission to share an observation. If he gives permission, gently share that you notice while his responses are welcome and helpful, they tend to be lengthy. Ask if it's possible for the person to be brief with his responses and to be mindful of giving others time to share. Remind him that it is a team effort to keep the group's discussion on track. This conversation will feel awkward and that's normal. You may feel there is someone else in the group that has a closer relationship with the person and can communicate the concern more gently or be better received. If so, remind your group member who is helping that the conversation he is about to have with the over-talkative person is confidential. This is important so not to embarrass the over-talkative member nor diminish his self-esteem.

Withdrawn Behavior. The person who displays this behavior isn't the one who is just quiet. I have had many quiet people in my small group, but there was always a difference between being quiet and being withdrawn. The withdrawn type of behavior is best displayed when a group member removes himself physically from the small group circle or is doing something other than what the small group is doing. I once had a gentlemen get up out of his chair during the middle of our Bible study and without a word walk to a room where there was a TV, turn it on, sit down in front of it and watch a football game with which he was obsessed. That's a lot withdrawn. It also made our group concerned about him. I sent someone back to check on him. Fortunately, the one I sent back didn't stay and watch the game with our withdrawn group member. Chances are that you will have quiet people in your group. It doesn't mean that they are withdrawn. Most likely they are still paying attention to the conversation, just watch for body signals like a little smile or a raised eyebrow.

When someone shows withdrawn behavior that is distracting to the group, you should address it sooner than later. Something is wrong. If the person leaves the room, immediately ask someone who knows the person well to go to the person and find out what is going on. Or if the person remains in the room, address the issue first in private after the meeting is over. If the situation involves the whole group then it could be brought back to the group. Regardless, it will require a conversation in which one first asks the person if he could talk about the issue, then second, begin to listen and try to help find a solution if it involves the small group.

Giving Advice. Giving advice is a bad idea especially when the person sharing just needs to talks. Usually an exchange of ideas is welcome during the small group discussion. The purpose of the Bible study discussion is to uncover biblical truth and how to apply it and therefore, an exchange is welcome. However, when someone brings a problem before the group, there will be as many opinions as there are group members present. Giving advice also tends to take the group further down the rabbit trail and will most likely make your group members uncomfortable.

To address this type of behavior I would be pre-emptive and already have this value written in your group's covenant and refer to that value in the discussion of your covenant. Remind the group why offering advice is not recommended in the group setting. I also don't let the conversation drag out. Once I feel the conversation has run its appropriate course, I ask the person sharing the problem if the group could pray for him and if he says, "Yes," then we stop and pray right there on the spot.

Using insider Language. Groups often form their own language after a few months. This is why it's good to keep focused on unconnected people. Also, church-eeze type words are not helpful. One church I was a part of had insider language such as "life-changing connection," "Choose Compassion," and "Relentless." Another church has insider language such as "know, grow, go," "i3," and "the seven strives." Each of these terms can be helpful, but they need explanation because they can mean different things to different people – even within those congregations. Small groups have insider language as well. The mention of someone's name can refer to a particular situation. Or, the name of an incident, such as "the crash," or "the campaign" may be foreign to newer group members.

The only way to keep it from being distracting is to recognize the insider language and give a brief explanation of the meaning behind the word or phrase for the benefit of everyone.

Diverging Behavior. This involves someone trying to take the discussion off track as often as possible in order to cover one of his or her "pet" topics—such as politics. Or it could be someone like me who simply loves to bounce around on topics that I find fun and entertaining. However, everyone in the group doesn't always find it as fun and entertaining as I do. It becomes very distracting.

What do you do? Like all the other types of disruptive behavior, it usually requires a conversation. I find that good conversations revolve around an evaluation of your group's covenant. While using or evaluating your group's covenant won't prevent disruptions from happening, it will help address boundaries and minimize the opportunity for issues to arise. Reviewing your group's covenant on a regular basis is the best prevention of most disruptive issues. Take out your small group covenant and evaluate as a group how you are doing. Take a section or a selected value at a time.

Rely on others in the group for help. You don't have to tackle each disruption on your own. It may just be that the best person to handle a difficult conversation is someone in the group who has a stronger relationship with the disruptive person than you.

Second, don't get pulled into the disruption yourself. It may look fun or you may want to play the role of counselor, but don't do it. Remember the rest of the group must go down the path with you if you do. That creates a whole bunch of uncomfortable people.

Third, don't take any conflict personally. The disruption generally isn't directed at you. The person brought it with them to the group meeting. They just needed to express it. Continue to show understanding and concern towards the person while you work at keeping the group on track.

Key Phrase to Remember:

Keep the group on track.

For Discussion

1. Which disruptive behavior do you think is the most challenging?

2. What are ways you have dealt with disruptive behavior in the past?

3. Which type of disruptive behavior are you most likely to fall prey to and how can you prevent yourself from behaving that way?

Chapter 11
Showing Ownership

SECRET #10

"If You Don't Show Ownership With Your Group, Neither Will Anyone Else."

Nikki's small group had been meeting every week for two months. The group had grown from 6 to 16 adults and was still growing. For those first two months, she alone led the group meeting. The positive momentum the group was experiencing was on her side. Then the demands of her job forced her to miss group meetings. In a two month stretch she missed every week and with each week she had the group decide the week before who would lead the next group meeting. Even though her small group knew she was at work, they began to wonder if there was an underlying reason she wasn't there. Even though work demanded she be away from her group, her group began to take it personally. They sensed that they were no longer important to Nikki. Subconsciously, her group questioned if Nikki had any ownership in her own group. The group began to wonder if the group itself could be sustained without a leader who could be at the meetings.

The first time Nikki returned to her group after being absent several weeks, one of the group members took her aside and said, "I know you haven't been able to be here much and you probably can't be here all the time. Would it be okay if I took on the leadership of the small group?" Nikki knew that she wasn't able to be at most meetings and that she didn't have as much time to give to the group. So she wisely and immediately said, "Yes," to the group member's request to lead the group. In that transition of her group's leadership, the new leader showed interest in the life-changing impact of the small group and they began to grow and thrive again.

Showing Ownership with Your Group

It is truly amazing how group members can sense when a leader is showing a lack of ownership. Without the group leader showing ownership in the group, enthusiasm for creating a life-changing small group will most likely not occur. I am amazed at how simple, yet so powerful showing ownership with your small group is.

There are two simple ways to prove your ownership with your small group. The easiest way to show ownership is to attend your own small group meetings. This sounds so simplistic. Yet, it is so true. Nikki's story illustrates so well the importance of showing ownership. Had it not been for the group realizing her inability to have ownership in the small group, the group would not have lasted.

The only thing worse than missing small group meetings is to come to meetings unprepared. Coming prepared to your group meeting is the second way to show ownership because your small group members can tell when you aren't prepared. Even trying to "wing it" doesn't pass the smell test when it comes to demonstrating ownership with your small group. Plan and write down on a sheet of paper the group meeting agenda. Use the sample agenda in the appendices as a first step; then take time to prepare the study and other group activities. Write on the study guide your answers to the questions and Bible notes as well.

Now, let's say you feel that you are failing at the above ways to demonstrate ownership with your small group. There is one more thing you can do that can help erase these failings. Contact your group members regularly between meetings. Give them a phone call. Emails and texts are great, but there is nothing that can replace the human interaction that takes place when a conversation happens.

Your small group members look forward to having a few moments to talk with you during the group meeting;

however, when you intentionally take time to call your group members outside the meeting time, they know you are thinking of them and that you care for them. At that moment, your group members aren't thinking how wonderful it is that you are showing ownership with your small group. They simply feel special and loved.

Key Phrase to Remember:

Show ownership in your group.

For Discussion

1. In what things do you feel you have ownership? How do you show it?

2. Describe the house of homeowners who take ownership in their home and property and homeowners who don't. Now describe it in terms of a small group.

3. Give some examples when ownership goes overboard.

Chapter 12

Do Small Groups Work?

Let's come back around to our original question; do small groups work? You bet they do! Let me tell you about our neighbor Ken. While I had been praying off and on for him and his wife, Jill, for some time, I didn't really know them well. One Sunday to my surprise, Ken's wife walks into our church's newcomers class. I never knew she had started to attend our church. I just happened to be teaching the class that day and had a sense of embarrassment because I never knew she was attending and *I* wasn't the one who invited her; however, I was glad she came. A few weeks later she gave her life to Jesus Christ. The only question on that exciting day was, "What about Ken?"

Ken is in the army and was deployed at the time. He had another six months remaining of his deployment. The question was, "How would Ken respond to her decision?" No one knew. Shortly after Jill's decision to give her life to Christ, she became a part of our small group. There is nothing fancy or splashy about our small group. We share what's happening in our lives, study the Bible together, and pray together. Shortly after Jill joined our small group, we began to pray for Ken. It wasn't that Ken needed it as if he was in dire need of prayer, but because we cared about him. We cared about him because he is Jill's husband, and she loves him. Almost every week we prayed for Ken's safety, fulfillment with his work, and that he would become a part of our group when he returned.

Six months later, Ken returned from deployment, but, he didn't come to our small group. So, we continued to pray. I remember one night after group Jill shared with us that Ken had agreed to go to church with her the next weekend. She was giddy to say the least. The next weekend came and Jill, Ken, and a friend of Ken's went to church, and we prayed that it would be a good experience. It was! Ken's life was changed forever and he gave his life to Jesus a few weeks later. The very next week, guess who came to our small group? Ken! He has blessed our small group ever since. Would Ken have given his life to Jesus Christ if our small group was not a part of the process? I don't know. But I do know that our small group played an important role in providing what was needed to support both Jill and Ken so that the Holy Spirit could work in Ken's life. So, do small groups work? Yes, but not because a few people simply meet and call themselves a small group. Small groups work when a safe place is created by fostering trust. When trust is present as the group moves through its agenda, the Holy Spirit has a place to work in people's lives.

For Discussion

1. What is one thing you hope your small group will be for your group members?

2. What can you do so that this hope is realized?

3. What is one thing you hope for yourself by leading a small group?

APPENDICES

Appendix A
Sample Small Group Agenda One

Always start and end on time.

- Opening Prayer (Two minutes)

- Opening Activity/Ice Breaker or Opening Question from Bible Study (10 minutes)

- Bible Study (50 minutes)

- Prayer Requests and Group Prayer (20 minutes)

- Group Business (8 minutes)

- Fellowship/Refreshments (Post meeting)

Other possible agenda items:
- Worship
- Outreach activities

A typical small group meeting lasts between an hour and a half to two hours. The times assigned to each agenda item will vary from meeting to meeting.

Appendix B

Sample Small Group Agenda Two

Always start and end on time.

- Worship (10 minutes)

- Prayer Requests and Group Prayer (20 minutes)

- Scripture Reading and Bible Study (50 minutes)

- Group Business (9 minutes)

- Closing Prayer (1 minute)

- Fellowship/Refreshments (Post meeting)

A typical small group meeting lasts between an hour and a half to two hours. The times assigned to each agenda item will vary from meeting to meeting.

Appendix C
Our Small Group Covenant

It's a good idea for every group to put words to their shared values, expectations, and commitments. A written agreement will help you avoid unspoken agendas and disappointed expectations. Discuss each item before the end of your first group meeting and modify anything you need to as you move forward. If the idea of having a written agreement is unfamiliar to your group, we encourage you to give it a try. A clear agreement is invaluable for resolving conflict constructively and for setting a path for good group health.

The purpose of our small group is to lead people to a closer relationship with Jesus Christ by . . .
- Knowing Christ
- Growing in Christ
- Going for Christ

We agree to the following expectations:
- This group will normally meet every:

- Actual meeting time is to begin at and end at

- We will meet at:

- Refreshments or meals will be handled in the

following manner:

- Childcare will be handled in the following manner:

We agree to the following values:

1. Priority. Because we believe in the value of community, we agree to give priority to the group meetings. If we are running late, we will call ahead.

2. Confidentiality. We agree that whatever is shared here stays here. This includes what is shared through phone calls, etc. We want this group to be a safe place to grow.

3. Participation. We agree to encourage, support, and stand behind one another, choosing to see ourselves linked together.

4. Accessibility. To give one another the right to call upon one another in time of need – even in the middle of the night.

5. Openness. We will seek to be open and honest with each other. Our small group is a place where we can remove our masks and be ourselves and where we are accepted for who we are.

6. Respect. We agree to communicate in ways that are respectful and give advice only when it is requested. We will strive to be available to one another and listen, encourage, support, and tell the truth in loving ways. We agree not to confess anyone else's sins except our own.

7. Open Chair. We agree to keep an empty chair for others and seek to reach out to people like us who need this place of caring and growth.

Appendix D
Childcare Evaluation

Rate on a scale of one to five your group experience in regards to childcare. Then talk about ways your group can improve weaknesses and maintain strengths.

1. **Distractions: Consider noises, loud toys and activities, and movement through the house.**

1	2	3	4	5

I can hear the children more clearly than I hear our group leader.

It's so quiet. We have children here?

2. **Discipline: Consider hitting, biting, disobedience, how discipline is handled, and the parents' role in discipline.**

1	2	3	4	5

I can't look sternly at a child without getting in trouble with his/her parents.

I have permission to direct and keep every child safe from harm.

3. **Children's Perspective: Consider who's in charge, host home rules, where children play, and clean up.**

1	2	3	4	5

The kids think they are in charge.

The kids have heard, understood, and follow the ground rules.

4. **Resources: Consider activities for children and access to cleaning supplies.**

1	2	3	4	5
The kids are on their own. They're not our problem.			Our childcare can be described as purposeful and well supplied.	

5. **Childcare Workers: Consider job description, training, compensation, and appreciation.**

1	2	3	4	5
We need childcare for our childcare worker.			I would like to personally adopt our childcare worker.	

6. **Location: Consider where, boundaries, and safety.**

1	2	3	4	5
The kids might as well be playing in the street.			The setting for childcare is safe and well-equipped.	

7. **Cost: Consider whether you're paying the right amount.**

1	2	3	4	5
It's breaking the bank!			There's money left to take my spouse on a date!	

Remember that if your group provides childcare, it will be one of the most sensitive and personal things your small group does. It also as the potential to be one of the most impacting aspects of your small group. The evaluation you just completed is intended to start discussion rather than be indicative of how childcare may or may not be going in your small group.

Top Two Areas of Growth in Childcare:

1.

2.

Top Two Areas to Maintain Strength in Childcare:

1.

2.

Appendix E
10 Secrets of Small Groups that Work

1. **Develop a plan for your small group launch**. Using simple steps in starting a small group will increase the chances of success and keep your plans on track. Always start with step one.

2. **Create an environment of trust**. Group members will grow best when their relationships are built on trust. Without trusting relationships, what is learned in a group is only head knowledge. It takes two people to form a relationship that can be built on trust.

3. **Welcome with acceptance**. Say, "There you are!" instead of "Here I am!" which takes away fears from group members. Three little words can make all the difference: "There you are!"

4. **Use a covenant.** It makes clear the purpose, guidelines, and values of the group. Four-getting to use a covenant is a mistake.

5. **Think white-water raft guide**. These five words give the small group a stake in the group's success.

6. **Ask good questions**. It takes 6 seconds to ask a question for a life-time impact. Life-change happens best when people discover biblical truth for themselves.

7. **Practice Accountability**. Seven is the perfect number. Accountability is the perfect way to encourage growth to move from an idea to a habit.

8. **Listen with understanding**. Listening is equally as important as talking because it affirms and builds trust. The number 8 without a beginning or end illustrates that good communication doesn't end with talking, it must be completed with listening.

9. **Keep the group on-track**. Keeping the agenda on-track will help keep group members' focus and interest. A 9 on its side looks like the eye you need to stay focused on your group's agenda.

10. **Show ownership**. Showing ownership in your group helps group members become more committed to your group. Whether you have 2 or 10 people in your group, showing ownership encourages all to have ownership.

Appendix F
10 Secrets of Small Groups that Work
Fill in the Blank Quiz

1. _____ __ _____ _____ _____ _____ _____ _____. Using simple steps in starting a small group will increase the chances of success and keep your plans on track. Always start with step one.

2. _____ __ _____ __ _____. Group members will grow best when their relationships are built on trust. Without trusting relationships, what is learned in a group is only head knowledge. It takes two people to form a relationship that can be built on trust.

3. _____ _____ _____. Say, "There you are!" instead of "Here I am!" which takes away fears from group members. Three little words can make all the difference: "There you are!"

4. _____ __ _____. It makes clear the purpose, guidelines, and values of the group. Forgetting to use a covenant is a mistake.

5. _____ _____-_____ _____ _____. These five words give the small group a stake in the group's success.

6. _____ _____ _____. It takes
   6 seconds to ask a question for a life-time impact.
   Life-change happens best when people discover
   biblical truth for themselves.

7. _____ _____. Seven is the
   perfect number. Accountability is the perfect way to
   encourage growth to move from an idea to a habit.

8. _____ _____ _____.
   Listening is equally as important as talking because it
   affirms and builds trust. The number 8 without a
   beginning or end illustrates that good communication
   doesn't end with talking, it must be completed with
   listening.

9. _____ _____ _____ ___-_____.
   Keeping the agenda on-track will help keep group
   members' focus and interest. A 9 on its side looks
   like the eye you need to stay focused on your group's
   agenda.

10. _____ _____. Showing
    ownership in your group helps group members
    become more committed to your group. Whether
    you have 2 or 10 people in your group, showing
    ownership encourages all to have ownership.

Appendix G
Small Group Leader Evaluation
10 Secrets of Small Groups that Work

Looking back and evaluating where you have been as the leader of your group will help you move forward. After, reading each of the 10 statements below, circle the number that you feel best describes your current status as the leader of your small group. The numbers closer to 1 indicate a possible growth area and the numbers closer 10 indicate a strength to maintain.

Remember that this assessment does not tell you what your group members think, so the pressure is off! This assessment only reflects what you think about your leadership of your group at this moment. This assessment is only a tool and not a test or indictment of your leadership. Who knows, you may score all 10's!

1. Develop a plan for your small group launch:

I am purposeful in planning not only for the next group meeting, but also for my groups plans for months down the road.

1	2	3	4	5	6	7	8	9	10

My group is
sputtering to start.

Even though my
group has started, I
still look for ways
to keep its
momentum.

2. Create an environment of trust.

I am facilitating my small group so that relationships continue to grow and are healthy.

    1   2   3   4   5   6   7   8   9   10

My group prays with one eye open.   My group shares their inner secrets.

3. Welcome with acceptance.

I feel to my best ability that I am fostering a group atmosphere of welcome and acceptance.

    1   2   3   4   5   6   7   8   9   10

There are still strangers in the room.   Its like Cheer's where everyone knows your name.

4. Use a covenant.

My group knows of and is reminded regularly of our covenant and what it says.

    1   2   3   4   5   6   7   8   9   10

I am not sure my group can say why we meet.   My group is on-focus and on-task.

5. Think white-water raft guide.

I am intentional at delegating and encouraging participation in our small group.

1	2	3	4	5	6	7	8	9	10

I feel like I do everything for my group.

My group jumps in accepting roles needed to be fulfilled.

6. Ask good questions.

I lead the discussion primarily through questions in order to gain as much group participation as possible and group ownership in Bible application and group life.

1	2	3	4	5	6	7	8	9	10

I prefer to teach and and tell the group how scripture is to be applied.

My group is fully engaged in scripture through my discussion questions.

7. Practice Accountability.

I not only remind my group of scripture application steps they decided to make from the previous Bible study lesson, but I also encourage group members to look for ways to invite accountability within the group.

1	2	3	4	5	6	7	8	9	10

I and other group members keep our spiritual health a secret.

My group members invite accountability within the group.

8. Listen with understanding.

I take time to listen carefully to what group members say and let them know through my words and body language that I am listening with understanding.

1	2	3	4	5	6	7	8	9	10

My earplugs work well!

My group members feel valued.

9. Keep the group on track.

I am aware when group members take our group agenda and discussion off track and I work to bring our focus back to the conversation at hand.

1	2	3	4	5	6	7	8	9	10

We love rabbit trails
and I haven't worn a
watch to group in weeks.

Our group is
sensitive to the
group's agenda and
honor other's time.

10. Show ownership.

I prioritize my time so that I attend every group meeting and come prepared to lead.

1	2	3	4	5	6	7	8	9	10

My group thinks I have
put our small group up
for sale.

My group can tell I
own the deed to
our small group.

Based on the evaluation results, consider which of the 10 Secrets in which you scored lowest. Which would you like to improve . Consider up to three steps you can take this next month to foster growth in those areas.

Don't try to work on too many at one time. Pick two or three to work on and spend time improving those secrets.

Secret on which to work:
My next steps:

1.

2.

3.

Secret on which to work:
My next steps:

1.

2.

3.

Secret on which to work:

My next steps:

1.

2.

3.

ABOUT THE AUTHOR

Mark Ingmire has a love for small group leaders and their growth. He has led small groups ministries in the local church for more than 20 years during which time he has led his own small group and has trained and mentored hundreds of small group leaders in small and mega-churches alike. Mark's wife, Margaret, is his biggest supporter. Together, they are blessed with two children, Collin and Olivia. Mark has written many articles for Christianity Today's smallgroups.com and has been an encourager for many small groups ministries. Mark serves as the Adult Discipleship Director at Forest Hill Church, South Park Campus in Charlotte, North Carolina.

www.ingramcontent.com/pod-product-compliance
Lightning Source LLC
LaVergne TN
LVHW021506080426
835509LV00018B/2417

9 781628 885309